WALTON WELL

CULTURE ART POETRY FICTION SOCIAL JUSTICE

PRESS

PRAYER FOR MY DAUGHTER

ALSO BY DAVID ST. JOHN

POETRY

Hush (1976)
The Shore (1980)
No Heaven (1985)
Terraces of Rain: An Italian Sketchbook (1991)
Study for the World's Body (1994)
In the Pines: Lost Poems, 1972–1997 (1998; 2016)
The Red Leaves of Night (1999)
Prism (2002)
The Face: A Novella in Verse (2004)
The Auroras (2012)
The Last Troubadour (2017)

LIMITED EDITIONS

For Lerida (1973)
The Olive Grove (1980)
A Folio of Lost Worlds (1981)
The Man in the Yellow Gloves (1985)
The Orange Piano (1987)
A New Shade of Blue (1998)
Peruvian Portals (2013)
The Window: Poems, 1998-2012 (2014)

PROSE

*Where the Angels Come Toward Us:
Selected Essays, Reviews, and Interviews* (1995)

EDITOR

The Selected Levis, by Larry Levis (2000)
American Hybrid: A Norton Anthology of New Poetry
(with Cole Swensen; 2009)
The Darkening Trapeze: Last Poems of Larry Levis (2016)

PRAYER FOR MY DAUGHTER

POEMS

David St. John

WALTON WELL PRESS
Los Angeles   Oxford

Cover art adapted from T. Sturge Moore's design that appears on the
cover of the first edition of *The Wild Swans at Coole* (1919) by W. B. Yeats.

Design & Typesetting: ash good

Theresia de Vroom
Published by Walton Well Press
Los Angeles | Oxford

Paperback ISBN: 978-1-964295-03-9

Library of Congress Control Number: 2024915590

WALTONWELLPRESS.COM

Contents

V. PRAYER FOR MORNING

CODA

*

Once more the storm is howling . . .

—Yeats

I.

PRAYER FOR MY DAUGHTER

PRAYER FOR MY DAUGHTER

What prayer becomes me now
As these times darken daily
Until sons & daughters grow as
Fragile as the wind along these
Ever-altering surfaces of a world
Ripping apart——& whose
Fault really this sorrowing
Of fathers drawing only maps
Of their own fears as whole
Cities begin darkening in ash
Shadows as uncertain as Blake's
Own wild consumptive city by
The Thames & as Vivienne
& I walked those mornings
By the Pacific along
The Venice boardwalk talking
Looking past the ocean beyond
Waves barely holding the horizon
& I knew I could never make clear
My thanks for how she'd stood
Her ground those times I dragged
My wreckage through the house
As she with forbearance & humor
Helped me take my time to find
Safe harbor she who'd lived
Those impossible years twelve

To seventeen in a town of
Old & new angels
Their drugs & nightmares—
The friend who'd slashed herself
& bled out or the boy who'd stepped
Onto his family's fifth-story terrace
& a few steps beyond embracing
An ending of a life he felt already
Past repair & soon across her body
New tattoos like elegant illuminations
Of some Victorian screen unfolding
Inscriptions of inked cursive
Words like fire walking
Flaring as she began turning away
From old friends who'd
Defined the closing perimeter
Of a vortex she'd left refusing to
Acquiesce to a killing dark as she rose
Free & I think how
Young she is to know & how long
It took her father to choose light
Over dark & one night
Listening to her d.j. her radio show
At midnight I heard her play Leadbelly
Singing "Where Did You Sleep Last Night"
A song I'd once thought she'd known

Only from Nirvana & then a Hendrix
Twelve-string acoustic bootleg
Then Bessie Smith songs I had no idea
She knew & loved living up in Arcata
Between the redwoods & the sea
Where she'd grown singular & strong
In the solace of herself
While building her own Arcadia
As the prayer I might once have hoped
To send into the storm became
This belated song owing its life
To her grace & tolerance arising
Now as simply as then with music
Playing between the redwoods & the sea

II.

ELEGIES

MZ ROX STEADY

At the club *Saint Charles* nobody could call her anything
      except the stage name she'd coined

For herself after seven shots of Chris Blackwell's killer rum
      —*Mz Rox Steady* & it had a beat

& pretty much echoed her stride along the uneven parquet
      stage & I know because

I was the one laying down a few liquid bottom bass lines & one
      night Stacey pointed to her & said *That's mine*

A few weeks later Stacey told me Roxy was just another fantasy
      stitched of dozens of hummingbirds in flight

& that's how Roxy left this world   one hummingbird at a time

THESE DAYS

. . . I had not forgotten them

—Jackson Browne

I think tonight I should write to you again about the lives
    we left behind along

Old streets we'd thought might carry us into a future

Beyond those days that broke like ours so meticulously built
    upon a tarot deck of random

Foreign films & Sleepy John Estes songs & a few vague promises

Nobody ever quite believed & I don't mean to sound cynical
    I just want to remind you

Of the sort of holy innocence once so glorious & unsophisticated

& naïve it's now grown irrelevant & obsolete   these days—
    & no more these days

Do I confess to friends how the night breaks to apertures of

Lightning as we all seem so content with our individual fates
    dressing up occasionally

In one nostalgia or another & I see again in the face of a friend

I've known 30 years a cold reflection of that day he suddenly
        became somebody else: & what followed:

The panic on his face as if a hand had reached to grasp his throat

& all of the air in that Roman piazza was suddenly sucked up
        into the ancient ruins around us

& my own blank gasp of one man being suddenly hit hard

In his clenched stomach again & again & hard again & maybe
        just for effect by God

Even one last time   again

YOUR FACE

I just noticed your face in a magazine though you
      know how rarely I read those

Magazines devoted to stylish celebrities yet you
      looked so lovely & so very happy by

The young actor with his polished cheeks & severe
      black hair slicked back & lips perhaps

Even more red than yours yet you seemed truly
      happy in the photograph's glazed light

& you were standing exactly the way you'd posed at
      dawn looking down from the deck of your

Mother's house on the Silverado Trail staring out
      across those gray webs of damp vineyards

& I think beyond those days when you knew you'd
      never want me in your life

& there you were in a magazine as lovely & calm
      as that morning I was beside you as day

Arrived with its lustrous last catkins of spring

GOING PLACES

I was spending a lot of time in Georgetown sometimes sleeping
      at Howie's upstairs guest room

& hanging out along M street where I kept getting mistaken
      for Patrick Dewaere

Since *Get Out Your Handerchiefs* was playing just up the street
      & I didn't get it until I saw Dewaere

In a picture from *Le Monde* wearing glasses identical to mine & who
      wouldn't want to be him

In those good days before the world closed in all around him & some
      suicides hit you exactly

At the umbilical knothole pretty much untying everything you thought
      you'd cinched up tight

In your valiant late 20s when everybody who was anybody promised
      you were really going places

THE EMPTY SCHOOL HOUSE
(Bolinas Snapshot, 1969)

On the high bluffs lately illuminated by wildflower
    —lavender & phlox & white daisy—
All making wild the blowing
                grass of the spring meadows
    where a schoolhouse stood empty
Left without its faint scent the sweat of children's bodies
    mixing with the dust of abandoned
Moldering books stacked on
                each of the desks & shelved
    along the low cases still lining
The walls & the blackboard which was truly black & framed
    like a window open to the night
& an almost antique map
                of the world one of those slowly
    drawn down to illustrate
The flattened circumference of the globe & those seas so
    dark a green it seems they might
Breed life all over again even
                right there on that stiff woven
    canvas & it is those continents themselves
That we still desire *their* shapeliness as sensual as any body
    surfacing suddenly from the sheets to turn
Naked in those recurring waves
                still recalling some volcanic
    sport of the previous lives & nights

Of seven stretched bodies & earthly light brazen temperaments

      bordered by the cool margins of the sea

Fragments of the whole broken

                    across the surface of our world

      ironed flat by curved conventions

& the mapmaker of these shifting memories we all carry wishing

      for some rare defiance for the revision

Of every fierce geology still wishing

                 only to be whole truly whole

      whole truly & truly as before

OPEN ROAD

Who is that man
No one in the diner asked

As they looked up only
Briefly from their breakfasts

To watch him walking along
The roadside on the narrow patch

Of loose gravel between the asphalt
Of the desert road & where

The Joshua trees & pinnacles began
& he swung the worn chocolate

Rucksack off his shoulder for just
A moment to reach inside

& pull out a black flute he'd bought
On the street in Barcelona

& though the diners at that
Moment could not see him

They could hear the sob
Of the *cante jondo* he played

One of the *siguiriyas*
He'd been taught in a stand of pines

By a man leaning against a gray
Cadillac by a silver trailer

Whose door had opened onto a boy
Who also held up a guitar

Only his had one newly broken string
& five yet unbroken roads

OF BEAUTY

I think Jacob said of the ladder
It was   *A Thing of Beauty*

Yet I'm not certain if he meant
Its luminous destination

Or the ladder itself as our vehicle
To such pure mystery

I'd heard the phrase spoken
First with certainty by my own

Father holding up a glossy drama
School photo of my mother

Lifted from his torn-ragged college
Scrapbook one day

& I read in an essay this same
Phrase referring to an elegant lie

In a famous novel by John Le Carré
—with whom I once had lunch

In Baltimore along with an amusing
Anonymous actress—

& my father when I told him this story
Called it an especially

Savory detail as he relished its mystery
Though as a boy I'd discovered

My mother had a way of telling stories
Without a certain objective

Reality that I could locate or quite
Confirm but I confess I was

Undisturbed by a few untruths
Offered with such original beauty

Of image & a flair for the magical
Honored more than fact

So perhaps what she left to me in
Death was beyond the bare

Recognition truth cannot always be
A thing of beauty just as a ladder

Reaching a story of forgiveness
Reveals at its end a thing of beauty

Remains a thing of mystery

LATE FAREWELLS

Academy, California

Now that we have at last
Entered this doorway

Step through each page
Exactly as if you were your

Own grieving ghost
The change of weather begins again

(She said of the rain approaching
Across sibilant skies)

Allowing us to believe a few last
Branches of memory sway lately

As quietly as the few seasons
We have left to live

My reticence is about forgiveness
& solitude perhaps remorse

Let my silence be moral   & mortal too
After all her letters recalled:

I always said I was hard to love
But I wish you'd have fought a little

Harder for me & next time you might
Find someone easier I mean

Someone not a tsunami of hopes
Not your own grieving ghost

I don't want you to think you know me
I want you to think one day

You might know me even if now
You're still unsure & if

One day things don't seem quite right
Stop a moment

Where you're waiting   & look: look:
It's my own shadow leaving

Your book split by light

A SKETCH OF MALLARMÉ AS ICARUS

—89 Rue de Rome

Approving night he'd painted his nails black as onyx
Like those of the altar boy who'd secretly dipped
     the tips of each long finger
Into the amphora of ash abandoned by the Phoenix

As she left in her haste for another late appointment
        in the sky above the coast of Crete
& along a charred mahogany console he'd queued up six
Tibetan singing bowls newly emptied of draughts

Of an oily water lifted from the never-reluctant Styx
     —no one's preferred passage
Of dreams vacant as those of Gods in icy myths arising
Gold as sunsets blazing then blackening to this night

Inking a slow opiate pupil in the zero eye of a single die
Tossed in the gaze of the bemused poet sketched by
        a friend with a bent feather quill nicked off
One wing of some silent boy flaming to a final allegorical

Mirror of himself

III.

REQUIEM

REQUIEM FOR THE LOST SEASONS

In the Mojave heat moved like a fever
through light as if the dusk promised
another lake just ahead another body
of palms whipped by a last new moon
night's fanfare of black ribbons hung
along Moroccan mirrors & false pearls
their final embers gathered into songs
& folded within the melody those lyrics
of sleep laced by a scent of tombs as fog
follows along the narrow trails leading
up the canyon as silence again collapses
along the creek below erasing your desire
for day's tangle of rain salt & heat rising
off the mirages yet a lazy raven remains
its listless irony one of the few pleasures
slowly crushing you setting you adrift once
more what happens to the promises made
in the rainy season what happens to sworn
revelations after the muddy fields dry what
happens if white blossoms of almond orchards
shiver & storm across ravines at the edges
of this desert blinding those drivers making
their ways home to other cities & other lives
to lies told within those lives told & repeated
to friends you know O you know those lies
I mean you know those lies you know what
happens to those seeds of California poppies

& the wild foxglove you've held in your hands
through this winter of raw abstinence saving
these precious seeds so they may be at last
scattered across your garden & caught by these
blood-scorched winds beneath the late May sky

LIVES OF THE COMPOSERS

It begins with an acoustics of the mind a slight
shift in the trajectory of your thought walking
to your weekly lesson one late winter morning
in Vermont & standing before that oak door of
your elderly teacher looking up to a wide beam
above the porch watching a single drop forming
on the icicle hanging just above the steps & as
you listen to another student singing the passage
of *Orfeo* you've always loved & as slowly her
voice rises you see the drop has swollen a globe
a whole note lit silver in the morning light now
transparent as you step up onto that first step
lips beginning to open as if you were yourself a
single head afloat in a swirling river yet singing
still as the drop falls toward you as if all mystical
spheres were collapsing to a solitary world of song
the perfect bone skull bead falling from the mala of
a Tibetan monk a simple thing you've been born to
receive wholly & intact without regard for the quaint
immature physics of your century yet appropriate to
the bone moon setting tonight over the desert prophet
whose hymnal of the infinite seduces Sedona's alien rain

OCTOBER ÉTUDE

At night the chords soften to grays & blues rising again
to gather within this emptiness just as last October
I sat at an old upright piano in the darkened recital hall
after my daughter's final rehearsal & I felt those chords
moving through my body as I began playing to memory
just as when I was a boy looking out a picture window
of my teacher's living room where her Steinway
presided & I felt its majestic vibrations shuddering with
an A minor 7th opening chord to a movement forgotten
in my dream while the audience savored the silence
following & I froze mid-passage knowing even then it was
the certainty of music returning to the body I'd always
loved most as nature lifts us out of our silences those
few consolations of mystery inscribing a score for any
final recital we'll learn to perform alone at the worn keys
of an upright like this one in this dark rehearsal hall its
xanthic keys still shining where those soft fingertips
of an elderly accompanist had paused each time the ballet
mistress lifted her hand slightly to adjust some young
dancer's limb akimbo & then again fingers to the keys
as every night delivers us to the stars outside assembling
their mandalas & I think of times I'd walk the beach sands
feeling again the ways the weave of one's wasted light
draws tight the cirrus across the closed dome of night
framing in the sky's singular transience its constellation
of lucent scales of an albino dragon slain by St. George
as the October étude lifts us into our final transparence

THE SCULPTOR

He'd lived among the gold pages of the valley
its black veins its roads lacing the too familiar
fields just as the Sierras became a few abstract
shapes set against the stone sky he was alone
there always waiting to be recalled by God his
face in shadow & then something sudden in
an unexpected touch something he'd later tried
to remember for a whole year after the fabric tore
showing a saintly future something sweet felt at
that moment when the ice blackened beyond his
headlights as a few anonymous cypress opened
for him their crossed limbs & what could he say
to anyone that might be more eloquent than those
words he'd already spoken & what did he believe
he could still hold onto & what treasure might free
him from the world's measure or the smell of his
mother's skin as he knelt in mourning saying aloud
*I love the chisel's certainty less than I love this cold
stone* yet he remembered the roads along the spurs
of the Sierras stretching the whole eastern edge of his
valley & those childhood questions with no answers
left to be claimed & those silences he'd held long after
her body faded into the dark & also his final friend
until at last he alone remained by death unnamed

ABSINTHE IRONY & ALCHEMY

Tomaž wrote from Prague that some
loved absinthe & some irony yet mostly
he loved alchemy these days & he'd seen
black Mercedes sedans like roaches crawling
through the streets of Prague & puppets
praised the State though only marionettes
were loved by his friends & just past
the electric green lettering on the window
of an absinthe shop was the studio of an
old marionette maker he knew & a devil
danced with a child-sized mouse carved of
linden wood each hooked on a white metal
ladder & Tomaž wrote it'd all synced in his
mind with the alchemist Edward Kelly who
served The Castle 300 years before Kafka
lived on Golden Lane & Tomaž said one day
as he passed below Kelly's tower his own life
doubled by a nearby lake as ash green as Kelly's
suicidal aperitif of poisoned absinthe or those
tanks of a time not long before that icy irony of
Wenceslas Square transmuted by the bodies
of young alchemists sprawled across their fallen
books & that evening's newly blackening snow

GIULIETTA IN TRASTEVERE

It wasn't what I'd expected when I saw
the address Marco had written on the flyleaf
in my copy of Montale's *The Storm* (it really was)
just before we'd left his brother's bar next door
to a vacant dry-cleaning place on Broome Street
as he said *You've got to check in on her for me*
you've got to see how she's doing—you've
got to see if she's alive & I swore it would be
the first thing I'd do when I got back to Rome that
I wouldn't let a day pass before I'd go & see
Giulietta & that I'd call him right away to reassure
him those needles she'd loved hadn't lifted her
into some purgatorial silence & Marco was still
staring at me & saying nothing at all until just
a quick *I know you will* & it was only a few weeks
later I was back in Trastevere at Raphael's when
Giulietta entered the party as if dressed in layers
of silk & frost drawing every eye in the room to her
faux jaguar jacket hanging off bare shoulders & I saw
it wasn't an entrance so much as an accusation
aimed at the conversations in that room including
the one I'd been having about the movement of
the triangle in Kandinsky & its delicate mystical
agency with a Benedictine monk visiting Rome
from a high desert monastery at Valyermo where
I'd walked the Stations of the Cross one Good Friday
of a very bad year & now Raphael's party for our New

Year of more brutal fears had us all a little edgy with late
resolutions meant to resonate across a next World War
& soothe those nightmares awaiting us even though we
knew the truth was simply that nobody saved anybody
just as I'd never save Giulietta & love fades to *noir* in
every mercury mirror & all in all I think I was relieved
to see her coming over to me rings chiming a wine glass
as she moved next to me to say   *& so I see I'm just in time*

IV.

THE SKETCHBOOK

THE SKETCHBOOK (I)

Let's begin with these scales
Of gold light riding a script of leaves
& ferns twisting along
The antique boulevard as it
Swings suddenly to pass below
The old palazzi
Stacked up against the hillside
Red tiles lit by late afternoon sun
The blonde & amber stones
Trembling almost shifting a little
In the heat & glare as
The boulevard angles off again
This time down to the beach & rocks
& sea beginning to rustle
Just as the tides come in to brush
The hunched shoulders of the seawall
Along the strand of white sands
Where he paused to pick up a stone
The size of a marble & shaped like
An egg
Its base green as kelp yet
Veined with an electric yellow & at
Its bald tip a ridge of rose not
Scarlet but the dull red
Of clay ran marking the randomness
Of stone

Even this one she'd drawn

In her sketchbook after they'd walked

Out that afternoon along the seawall

To an abandoned

Lighthouse—a dead heron sprawling

Across the flagstones of the path—

& in her

Sketchbook she caught its exact collapse

Paying precise attention to broken

Feathers as they fell

So awkwardly across each other or

Stood singly in gusting Mediterranean

Winds & on that same page as

The stone she'd once

Begun a sketch of him leaning

Above the heron & with a stick lifting

One wing as

A cloud of penny-colored flies ascended

Out of the bird's open breast rising

Quietly & gathering

Around him like his own shadow

In the last light of the still waning Sicilian

Summer sun & it was then

He recalled the day at a small *papeterie*

Off Rue du Cardinal Lemoine

Its violet awning & its front window filled

With an extravagant display of

Marbled Florentine

Endpapers fanned out against

A dove gray cloth like a spread peacock's

Tail & it was there he'd bought her

The sketchbook its cover a deep red

The patient

Shade of blood one sees

Only on a butcher's apron at day's end

& this sketchbook

Became the single thing they

Shared each day outside of speech

This daybook of occasions they'd handed

Back & forth across

The table or bed each of them leaving

For the *other* drawings & notes

& overheard asides to be discovered

By the *one*

& the sketchbook slowly filled with

Pencil shadows & a pen's

Smudges & spiraling charcoal hieroglyphs

& fragments of stories —lines of

Interrupted lyrics or letters begun on

One page one day to be

Completed days later on another whole

Passages describing

Miniature parks or town squares
& stone towers or meadows & those
Meandering walks
Along the broken bricks of an ancient
Destitute & serene walled city or
The prospects of a mustard-lit countryside
& those urban grids & her vertical
Series
Of brown & violet
Ink drawings of a blank & derelict
Renault factory & its ruined collapsing
Steel presses——

                       & then one night
She entered into her old dream of
That childhood canal leading north forever
As it silently froze as
She the swimmer of the dream grew
Minute scales of
Ice upon her eyes & her lids closed
As the sky hunched above her like Cerberus
Asking   *Where are you going now*
No one else has ever gone?—— & that next
Morning the patchwork paisley
Gypsy duffle already packed & awaiting
Her by the hotel room door she
Looked up just as he

Placed a small white espresso cup

Before her on the wood table

As empty as the page beneath her hand

THE SKETCHBOOK (II)

After she'd left him only
The sketchbook remained holding
Its scent of passage & its fragments
Of scripts of a future
That would never be lived not now
No elevated passions not even those
Incidental scenes in the endless rooms
Of random *pensione* beside the stairways
& fountains marking
The shifting stages of their days & not even
A few pages of sunlight would fall open
In the mornings along
Her apartment floor the chaos where
She'd tossed the sketchbook onto a pile
Of telegrams streaked brown by dry
Red wine & congratulations about her
Last "triumphant" show of paintings
& photographs & she began to hate
Those pages where
She'd taped
Matchbooks & old *biglietti* & scrawled
The addresses of strangers below drawings
Mottled by weather & sweat

          just as she'd
Hated how in those last weeks as
They walked

In those cities they'd erased with every
Step the already fading & indistinct
Lines of a story they'd once drawn nightly
Until nothing was left but a naked
& weary present tense—
Virgin again & blank never to be remarked
Upon & as undefined as the scroll of
White birch bark
Nailed to an old friend's cabin wall
As a day's fire died against the stone hearth
Of what she'd claimed as her studio
& snow began
Again to fall as it had always fallen just
Beyond the winter windows of her father's
House just down the country road
& now it was falling beyond her & she
Thought how hard she'd grown
Even in her most envied virtues
Suspicious of everything she'd once
Wished for herself
                              those days back at the lake
Below her father's ramshackle barn her charcoal
Sketches & watercolors back then clarifying
Every page of visions including one
She'd claimed of art's true cross
At the still distant edge of

Possibilities without

Horizon & she said aloud *I wish*

I could see you as I saw you

Then I wish I could see you I wish

Again I could hold something of you

Who you were when you stood

At the end of the lake's small pier you

& those actual loons who like you

Cried across the dusk I wish I could see you

As myself seeing you

                      & a fox like a single

Brushstroke of burnt umber smudged

The erratic green of the far hedge

Marking the boundary

Of the fields of the neighbor's house & it

Was so simple almost like an afterthought

Or one of those elaborate inked

Margins of a rare Book of Hours in her father's

Library each beloved by him

As she loved

All marginalia & now only fragments

Still mattered to her only the minutia of

A life she began to learn again

In negative from the years of undeveloped

Frames as each day she'd print dozens

Of images from those rolls of

Black-&-white she'd found boxed & forgotten
In her narrow apartment back in Fells Point
Seeing again the sobriety of a defeat
She'd measured in those bodies ghosted by
Gestures & by every course of flesh she'd
Loved & touched even those few minutes
She'd despised every lesson she'd once
Refused every oak floor she'd paced as
Nervously as bougainvillea set trembling by
A rising breeze or that neurotic stem
Of blushing fuchsia in a glass vase or those delicate
Limbs of forsythia
All whipped nerve-endings blazing
As she held her breath until it passed that
Feeling of knowing if she did not open
Her aperture to the world it could
Not be admitted it could only *exist* & so like
So many things in this life she felt she'd once
Understood & lost she felt again fully:
No one plans to be a bride of nothing
Left in some burnished husk of one's own voice
Knocking in the skull or a breath drawn so
Violently no one else
Might share the night air—sometimes
Groping for any sign of any individual grace like
Those Parma violets

She'd tossed across the sheets to him while
She was thinking even then of another life
That one day she'd decide to live beyond him—
A life where at last she might indulge her love
For ruins & imperfection & finally resist
Imagination & so resist as well
That hateful nostalgia for an old sketchbook
& instead never recall again the broken story
Its raw its lost its irredeemable past

THE SKETCHBOOK (III)

After she'd left only
His faith in shadow & light
Remained as he traveled often
Nowhere he'd remember later
Though he began to see the ways
His life had become much less
Than met the eye as he passed
Through so many stories at last
He'd landed in Rome in late
March as a fierce mid-afternoon
Scirocco blew across Fiumicino
Its blood-red sand swirling across
Open doorways of the arrival lobby
Spilling dust of a hellish hourglass
Scraping beneath his scarred boots
& as he stepped out into
A consoling chaos of taxis & voices
He saw Antonio's sweet driver
Stefano waiting for him & yet also
Waiting for her—& Stefano
Raised one eyebrow with
The simple not unkind question
Dove la signorina? . . . not knowing
He had no answer & he looked away
As Stefano put one hand on his
Arm saying . . . *Mi dispiace* . . .

& as Stefano drove toward the city
He'd cranked down the window so he
Could smell the diesel mixing with
The dust a reminder he was returning
Along the Viale Trastevere
& Via Morsoni then Via Dandelo & up
Long sweeping turns
To Via Nicola Fabrizi & that faded
Rust-mustard house where Antonio'd
Lived during those years they'd first
Together sketched out scripts & he'd
Learned ways Antonio would give
Lives & language to his stories just as
He began to understand what it might
Mean to write with light & brush
With shadows the fields & the faces
Of a film unfolding like a fan the way
Waves might scrawl sheets of sand
Before a beach then retreat & returning
Revise those pages erasing hieroglyphs
Left by pipers running from the tides
& in those days his shoulder bag
Hung weighted down with his dented
Pawn shop Olympus & a sketchbook
To note both the seasons & the light
Meticulously logging each roll he'd shot

Adding pencil shadings beside his notes

& drawings to frame a future for

His stills stopping

Time first with images & fragments of

A new world arising as he began making

A few portraits of Antonio's friends

Those soon famous yet still raw in

Their beauty actors & fashion's bones

Frail Milanese mannequins & the drug

Debris of London those leftover lovers

All blazing together toward a time

They'd be lost to a disparate miscellany

Of failures yet he'd held each in

Such sharp focus in their rapturous

Frenzy & dissolute sexual prime frozen

In black-&-white prints framed on

Gallery walls & printed in newspapers

Then those nostalgic books all images

Of Antonio's circle those icons

Of a rare past illuminated by

An instant or a sudden shifting

Sleight-of-hand his stroking of

The light like feathers along the film

Light moving like fingers down a face

Along a body revealing its script of flesh

Of fortune & its circus of circumstance

Those resident mortal intimations of light

Gathering in a lens as memory itself asks

To be not so instantly *the past* leaving

The mind shuffling its lost

Reflections of the self yet perhaps this

Was what he too seemed like to Stefano

Now Antonio was dead just another of

Those once-beloved friends arriving

Back like the ghosts they were to gather

Final traces of who they'd been when

They'd gathered at Antonio's & the light

Moved toward its golden hour in the lens

& he was the final phantom arriving

At the door alone . . . yet it was she

Who'd first introduced him

To Antonio at *Taverna Trilussa*

Where he'd been sitting outside

At a metal table sketching in his

Graph-paged schoolboy's notebook

& he'd looked up as they'd passed

Through the small piazza

On their way to meet friends at

Da Gildo & was surprised to see them

Double back & stand just by his table

& as she lifted her black cloche hat

He'd recognized the girl

At the *enoteca* off the *Campo dei Fiori*
He'd been talking with one evening
Only a little while before friends
Pulled her away & back into the night
& now she stood just beside
His table with one of those friends
& she said to him *Ciao Luce* & then
To her amused friend said *Antonio*
Luce is the boy you told me
I'd never find again & as they simply
Picked up their conversation he'd lifted
His camera to take the picture she'd
Later taped to one of their sketchbook's
Opening pages this image of the future
They would triangulate into fate—she
Looking away & Antonio with a shot glass
Held up to his eye as a bleary lens finder
Their own jagged histories soon
Revolving together—pieces of bottle
Glass & shards of mirror revolving in
The kino-barrel of Antonio's kaleidoscope
Set moving by *his* currents of light
Projecting into a world of fluent
Images Antonio's stories
Of harsh childhood reckonings &
The Po Valley sketched & stitched

By *her* recollections of landscapes

Crosshatched by abandonment at

The stone farmhouse above her family

Lake & possibilities again returned

With the boy she'd call *Luce* naming

His own future building cities of light

& brushing Antonio's vision in exact

Shades of disquiet & desolation as

He himself had known in fields

Of punishing heat & vines ripe with

Ignorance in a valley so like Antonio's

Where night came framing him in its

Unholy dark yet here he was with her

Now just up the street from *Trilussa*

A lucky boy tossing Antonio the bent

Oak triangle across that worn felt

Of the only pool table in Trastevere

Where soon they'd work as one the three

Aligning each with the other those inner

Geometries retelling stories of lives

They'd braid & make lucid & intimate

& she watched him lifting the rough cue

As Antonio called the shot in English

An impossible 8 *on the break* & as the black

Planet spun into its pocket his luck lit the way

THE SKETCHBOOK (IV)

Did anyone believe one life mattered
More than any other or that lives
In a sketchbook held anything
Beyond a few gestures caught out of time
Always more by accident than by design
He was ready by then to be wrong about
Everything lit by a circus of public light
& in those years after they'd left Antonio
& Rome their friends remarked how
They'd always seemed to live for art
Faith beauty wreckage ruins disaster
Their elegant ashes blown by necessity
Or betrayal within an old deep trinity
During those years they'd lived as
Two their belief in a sequence of cities
All giving way that night in Blois
& he felt only a few stories remain
Living in one's pulse always
Affirmed by absences striking chords
In the body as they learned of
Antonio's health first oblique notes
& asides at parties more salacious
Than any vital gossip & he saw
Some loved requiems some departures
& some a slow gathering of solitude
Circumstance & the desire to give

Up desire altogether

& for once simply to get on with things

To pick up again where one's life had left

The rails or been shunted onto some

Dead-end siding behind an abandoned

Poulain factory that once sent

The smell of chocolate & cinnamon into

The morning air yes that was a bad night

No last resurrection of twin lives fixed

Only within the pages of a sketchbook

Their single story of themselves a fiction

Never to be recovered or reconstructed

Never to be told except in reflection & never

To see each other ever again she said

Never *never* again

As she left the Hôtel Anne de Bretagne

Leaving on the bed as if in a movie Antonio's

Note taking a night train to Rome to be there

For his last days

*

It was something he'd remembered

His old friend the English countertenor

Sharing one day at lunch at the long

Walnut table they'd carried out

To the garden & set beneath the calm

Umbrella pines & it was a day so

Rich in autumn light a kind of silence

Resembling peace had settled over

The few of them there & in an elegant

Familiar voice the world knew his friend

Said to a woman by him in a plum

Leather jacket yet really to everyone

At the table how at some point all

Of it (referring here to

His own life) had become nothing

But a slow series of late farewells

Numbing valedictory concerts

With the ghosts of friends in the first

Rows each night—yet at the table

That afternoon what *he'd* remembered

Hearing so clearly in his friend's voice

Was the thin tenderness of evening rain

Falling upon the roof tiles of a house

Abandoned to silence   & he

Realized no one's ever good at endings

Not that anyone should be & this

Was entirely like coming to the close

Of a story you'd thought would be far

More clever at

Its end or those final pages of

A sketchbook one carried for years
Ready every moment with a Staedtler
Or charcoal stick to note whatever time
Might still be left in the world with
Lines of shadow light & circumstance
Or a few photographs clipped & copied
Or favorite songs of surrender so sensual
One could almost see the light like a thin
Whip snake uncurling along
The limbs of possibility in those sketches
Of one's own passage across the days'
Desires those passionate humors
& fields of summer light & how could
Anyone have imagined the parcel
She'd sent arriving out of the silence
She'd broken & packed with a dozen
Bent proofs of his old photographs
The sketchbook itself their very first
The one she'd taken with her from Blois
Delivered in a plain cardboard box
A rough casket
Their ledger of that past illustrated
By twin ambitions twisting & uncoiling
& as he leafed through unconstructed
Early days it was familiar & consoling
The *papeterie* by

The Hôtel des Grand Écoles
A drawing of Parma violets by a vase
& his favorite photo of Montale's house
In Monterosso taken with his T2
So perhaps those days hadn't always
Seemed a fiction & at times she thought
Of a lucky boy who was *Luce* & light
& for a moment memory was hope but
He found the days in Blois one Polaroid
Of a lovely breakfast garden where
At that exact moment she'd felt
Him lift the camera she'd turned away
Yet also those delicate sketches of
The resolute bleached brick warehouse
By the Poulain factory then
Indeterminate landscapes & interiors
Quiet as late Bonnard drawings
Then a shift in time & space
New England/the White Mountains
Tipped in photos of her father her
Brothers & an unknown man who
Held the child Antonia all posed
Above the land where her father's farm
Stood & he felt his hands calming
Even as the pages grew fewer & fewer
At the sketchbook's end

                                     & then a page

Crosshatched with minute lines of
India ink like a heavy screen door
Shut against a late August night &
Hesitant to find what came next
He lifted slowly the black screen to
Blinding perfectly white facing sheets
Two virginal untouched pages bare
As bone at the sketchbook's end not
Unfinished nor unspoken but
Fashioned to an immaculate silence
A final closed aperture & what he felt
Was so unlike anything he'd imagined
He might at that moment not
Confusion only the relief of rain passing
Not grief only a pure release—& week
After week on the gray steel table
By his desk he left open

                                 the sketchbook

Apart & naked at those untouched pages
Their rag paper soft as flesh fading
As if somehow much remained to be added
As if two mirrored doors still lay side by side
Gazing up like dazed lovers in an open field
Reflecting upon the implausible sky above

V.

PRAYER FOR MORNING

PRAYER FOR MORNING

I *Pasternak in the Rain*

Stay silent be opaque never unconcealed
As one's silence may remain the one sentence
Unviolated by time though in time it's true
Even stories erode like porous Baltic seawalls
Not from coarse fingers of salt nor bulk & bruises
Of storm-driven waves but vaguely veiled losses
Near a wanderer's morning churchyard fire
Where sycamores embrace its risen smoke thick
As this incense escaping from the censer swung
By an altar boy who's torn his last pair of wool pants
& the flesh along his inner thigh beneath on the bare
Nail bent at the cemetery gate while hurrying to Easter
Service the storm still gathering & moving near & he
Knows only to stay silent as a nail in the rain he fears

II *Overlooking the Cortile*

Late winter yet we stood at the open window
Its green wood shutters pushed back like wings
Against the walls of the ancient building
We stood at the aperture of the narrow room
Looking down onto the fountain in the cortile
Her old room now mine & she said nothing
Of the year she'd slept here
Knowing the Russian painter she loved
Was out somewhere on the streets of Rome
Walking with his Contessa every evening at dusk
As the grief of a *rossignol* ran down the stones of
The faded wall just outside her window & along the ivy
Seeping slowly as water from the lips of Orpheus

III *The Rain on Van Buren Street*

They'd scraped their years down to the spiritual
Bone in a second floor flat of an old Victorian
They'd made elegant by their desires a place on
That hill above the creek a house where her favorite
Painter had once lived it pleased them living there
Their few antiques lighting the tall windows at night

Walking down their curving drive to Van Buren
After our late dinner I'd stop at the road not quite
Ready to disappear back to my side of town
Where I'd lived that summer in a perpetual
Abstraction of absence displacement & disdain
I'd glance up one last time to see them framed still
In a light beyond their never-drawn curtains
Arguing over money opiates rain & last remains

IV *The Implications of the Sky*

I've lived so long now without my worn felt ephemeris
I've given away my well-bent deck of Dali tarot cards &
Those yarrow sticks beside the I Ching are budded with dust
Every day a deeper abandonment as the cruelty unfolds
My only foretelling will be the loss of your garden's perennials
No longer what once we might have said were the promises
Of each coming day unfolding in the implications of the sky

All gone now no matter any soft nakedness of the sun or brief
Faith branching across the horizon no we're always left alone
With a few fresh questions tested by blood or circumstance
Or the smug rage of lies bittering the old hollowness
Of deep childhood nights left unstarred yet constellated again
By the pitted hunger of family & others' elemental judgments
Regarding the final fictive & exhausted lost glories of our kind

V *The Indiscreet History of My Silhouette*

More & more these days old friends seem intent
To remind me there's still time to redeem
The indiscreet history of my silhouette & in truth
I confess how comforting this notion has become
& so tonight I've come back to your old house
At Venice Beach carrying a bottle of D'Yquem
Knowing you require a priceless gold wine as you

Toast our past quoting your single hero Denis Diderot
Reminding me I too was once *Simply young*
Blonde & heading for a breakdown & walking out
Onto your worn teak deck you point to the single star
Now visible in the night sky as if to inscribe those
Distances remaining still between the indiscreet history
Of my silhouette & those untouchable shores of Venus

VI *The Blue Light*

Where were you as the light descended & do you
Believe still it was the far western face of the Sierras
In a spring meadow off Tollhouse Road as you drove
Down to the valley & were you living still at the ranch
Or had you left already for the Mendocino coast wearing
The braided leather belt I'd made for you that last spring
Together I hope you were driving the old green GMC
Panel truck we'd used at the bakery for our deliveries

I heard you wrote your sister you hoped soon you might
Marry the angel Gabriel now your spirit was a blue lamb
I think your heart was helpless to such music even if you
Could recall kneeling to plant those indigo iris by the path
To our cabin yet light brings so many inflections of beauty
Wasn't there anything at all you mourned of the leaving?

VII *Prayer for Morning*

after Voltaire

Beyond our prayers for morning beyond all mourning
    We watch auroras of past lives unfolding
These shifting fluent currents of the light illuminating
    Every last sad science of the night
As we look up again into the black wreck of the year
    Stunned by the wreckage of the light
Trying to reflect again how sometimes late in a life
    These lights might take us by surprise now
Nothing's left beyond those skies & we've been told
    How unwise to think of touching any
Constellation of regrets or embracing the familiar lies
    Lacing our myths across the dome of the sky
Even this sad science of night at times denies how late
    In our lives love took us by surprise

CODA

A NAME

Please stop a moment I know you are
In a hurry but I've been standing here
By the gate just waiting for you as I have
Something I've meant to give you for so

Long I'm sorry it's taken all these years
It's not much just this leaf of papyrus
A scrap of parchment a simple wafer to
Place on your tongue on which is written

A name you will taste as it dissolves so
Lift a glass to your lips it's a fine year for
Reds especially my vines along the banks
Of Lethe there's nothing more I'm asking

You to recall nothing I'm asking nothing
Please use the name anywhere you wish
For any reason even to book passage & cross
The Styx or to bribe your saints into silence

Please use it quickly I'm told its currency
Is fading & perhaps ignore the things you've
Heard words mean as we know words mean
Nothing now to anyone just allow the old music

To sleep on your lips a moment as your tongue
Tastes what dying does to clarify the song
& I know now I've passed through something
Though not quite yet beyond so I'm not speaking

From the other side no I'm still here although
I'm feeling cold if not yet cold as stone nor
As sands chilled by morning tides just a final
Page with only a few letters left to be inscribed

Notes

ELEGIES

These Days: *for Liam Rector*

Going Places: *a film by Bertrand Blier*

The Empty School House: *for Richard Hassell*

Open Road: *for Ralph Angel*

Of Beauty: *for Phyllis Jane Fries*

Late Farewells: *for Roberta Spear*

A Sketch of Mallarmé as Icarus: *Mallarmé's "Ptyx"; for Larry Levis*

REQUIEM

Requiem for the Lost Seasons: *for Howard Norman & Jane Shore*

The Lives of the Composers: *for Norman Dubie*

October Étude: *for Vivienne*

The Sculptor: *for Sam Pereira*

Absinthe Irony & Alchemy: *for Tomaž Šalamun*

Giulietta in Trastevere: *for Ilaria Caputi*

THE SKETCHBOOK

The Sketchbook: *for Italo & Ester Calvino*

PRAYER FOR MORNING

Pasternak in the Rain: *for Bruce Boston*

Overlooking the Cortile: *for T.*

The Rain on Van Buren Street: *for Barbara Campbell*

Prayer for Morning: *for Anna*

CODA

A Name: *for Susan Terris*

Acknowledgments

Blackbird: "Going Places"

The Georgia Review: "Requiem for the Lost Seasons; October Étude; A Name"

Great River Review: "Prayer for Morning" (as "A Reflection")

The Kenyon Review: "Mz Rox Steady"; "These Days"; "The Sketchbook (I)"

Los Angeles Review of Books: "Of Beauty"

The New Yorker: "Prayer for My Daughter"

Nine Mile: "Pasternak in the Rain"; "Lives of the Composers"

Poem-A-Day (The Academy of American Poets): "Overlooking the Cortile"

Prairie Schooner: "The Sketchbook (III)"

The Southern Review: "The Sketchbook (II)"; "Late Farewells"; "Absinthe Irony & Alchemy"; The Sketchbook (IV)"

Spillway: "The Empty School House"; "Your Face"; "Open Road"

Throughlines: "The Implications of the Sky"

Washington Square Review: "The Rain on Van Buren Street"

The Yale Review: "Giulietta in Trastevere"

"The Sketch of Mallarmé as Icarus" first appeared in both the exhibition and catalogue of Martinez Celaya's retrospective SEA SKY LAND: *towards a map of everything* at the USC Fisher Gallery.

About the Author

David St. John has received The Rome Fellowship and The Award in Literature, both from The American Academy of Arts and Letters; the O. B. Hardison Prize from The Folger Shakespeare Library; and the George Drury Smith Lifetime Achievement Award. He is the author of many collections of poetry, most recently, *The Last Troubadour,* as well as a prose collection entitled *Where the Angels Come Toward Us.* David St. John has written two libretti: for the opera based on his book, *The Face,* by Donald Crockett, and the choral symphony, *The Shore,* by Frank Ticheli. He was also co-editor of *American Hybrid: A Norton Anthology of New Poetry.* A past chancellor of the Academy of American Poets and a member of the American Academy of Arts and Sciences, David St. John is University Professor and Professor of English and Comparative Literature at The University of Southern California.